THE LOST THIRD OF OUR LIVES

THE LOST THIRD OF OUR LIVES

Poems

EDWARD L. ALBAN

Alban Books

CONTENTS

Dedication	viii

1
ON SLEEP AND DREAMS — 1

Transcendental Sleep	2
The Blessings of Awakenings	3
Sleep's Pelagic Voyage	4
Sleep's Oneiric Stage	6
Sleep's Dark Interludes	8
Of Sleep and Death	10
The Transnighter	12
Drowsiness	13
Insomnia	14

2
SLEEP: THE LOST THIRD OF OUR LIVES — 15

Accounting for Sleep	16
Do Unremembered Dreams Have Value?	18
Remembered Dreams	20
Inner Echoes of a Poetess in a Mathematician's Body	22

Self-Reflections in Dreams	23
Art in Dreams and Dreams as Art	25
Daydreams	33
Sleep's Mysterious Memory	35
Stealing Dreams	37
Sleep's Magic	40
Dream-Making	43
Encounters with Conscience	47
Games Conscience Plays	49
Can We See Conscience While Awake?	51
Oracles and Prophecy	53
Muses	55
The Fabulists' Muse	58
Ravel's Muse	60
JFK: May 21, 1961	62
The Real World in Dreams	65
The Alarm Clock	66
An Ode to the Bed	68
Some of the Characters Cast in Dreams	70
The Books of Life	71
And Finally, the Why of Dreams	72
About The Author	74

Copyright © 2024 by Edward L. Alban

All rights reserved. No part of this book may be reproduced in any manner whatsoever without written permission except in the case of brief quotations embodied in critical articles and reviews.

First Printing, 2024

For Elizabeth

ON SLEEP AND DREAMS

Transcendental Sleep

Before birth, the sleep of the womb.
Beyond death, the sleep of the tomb.
From sleep to sleep we go
Life shining for a second and then lo
Just blinking like an errant blip
Between sleep and sleep.

Our time awake is only a spark
Amidst eternities of dark
While death and sleep
Are given eons to keep.
Why shouldn't a life so brief
Cause ire and grief?

The Blessings of Awakenings

Because each day upstages death
With blossoms of rebirth
Because each splendid dawn
Proclaims that we're not done
And dark of night makes way
For yet another day.

Awakenings have hints of immortality
Distracting us from our fatality.
Rebirth is constantly on its way
Renewing life with each new day.
In 20 years, we rise to thousands of tomorrows
Obliterating transcendental sorrows.

The sense of life becomes so strong
We never dwell on death too long.
As for sleep, it's only a temporary rest
To energize life's quests.
At times it seems a waste of time
At times a thing sublime.

Sleep's Pelagic Voyage

It is a nightly journey we traverse
On sails of sheets and pillows
Across a sea of darkness
Enroute to an undiscovered island
In the archipelago of tomorrows.

We disembark upon a bright new day
Recharged, awash in sunlight
And carry on about our chores
We work, we eat and drink
And never think about sleep
The sea that brought us there.

Until the day is spent
Until the island is on fire
Its flames surrounding us
And forcing us to flee.

It's then we seek the dark
Mysterious passage to salvation
The dark blue sea of rest
Our exit from a day in flames.

We reach a pier along the shore
An embarkation point to new beginnings
It is our bedroom
And moored to it we spot our bed
She's like a bright and white

Beautiful ship
About to take us to
The splendor of a fresh
And green tomorrow.

Sleep's Oneiric Stage

They could have made sleep
A dull and banal bodily function
A time for maintenance
A coma, a void that mimicked death.
But no, they added dreams
And made of sleep a treat
A sumptuous feast at the table of rest
An outing for the soul in the expanses of the mind.

The body rests with shuttered eyes
And then the mind trots out a world
Where nothing is forbidden
And nothing is impossible.

Before man heard of Hollywood, or Broadway
Before TV or internet, man relished dreams
And they were magical!
Before the days of drugs
Of herbs and mind expanders
Before exotic yoga and transcendental meditation,
Our sleep provided more than rest or entertainment,
Embodying the requisites for health and rehabilitation.

Before ghost movies or spooky flicks
Of Dracula or Frankenstein
We had nightmares that haunted us
In which we saw the dead.

And we had psychic dramas
Where conscience put us through a ringer
Rebuking us for sins and broken promises and pledges.

We also had cartoons and Disney fare
Sublime and wondrous Heaven-crafted plays
Where we were actors, audience,
Composer and director and playwright.
We were made kings of realms
In fantasies that brought us comedy,
Romance, suspense, and thrills.
In worlds of dreams all wishes were fulfilled
And man's shortcomings were corrected.
There were no poor, nor misbegotten ones.
There were no infirm or weak or disaffected ones.
We all possessed the faculties and virtues
That privileged ones possessed.
The poor felt rich,
The blind discerned the gift of light
And all for just the measly price of snores.

Upon returning to the daily rut
We felt enriched,
Rejuvenated by sleep.
The lonely might still be lonely
But not so disaffected
The poor will still be poor,
But much emboldened to follow course and not despair.

In dreams we met with fairies
And chatted with our guardian angels,
With muses, oracles, and patron saints.
They showered us with hope and inspiration
They gave us talent and special aptitudes
A singing voice, an ear with perfect pitch
A sharp discerning eye, a heart, a brain, a soul so grand
That made our mundane world more heavenly.

Remarkably, all this may well have taken place
Upon the unremembered dream of one forgotten night.
But no one can deny it happened!
How else to explain the fairy's gift that is so real,
That still endures, and it is ours to keep?

    Z   z   z   z   Z

Sleep's Dark Interludes

Sometimes while we're asleep
Our brain is partly anesthetized
And we don't dream at all.
We live in depths
Of unawareness so deep
We mimic
The nullity of not being.

Are we in a cave? A tomb?
Five thousand leagues under the sea?
Could be all of the above.

We are, for sure, in triple darkness:
A room completely dark
With eyes completely shut
And mind in dreamless sleep.

But who needs eyes to see what isn't there?
Who needs the sense of touch
To feel the nothingness of nothing?
And darkness isn't sinister
And blindness isn't dreadful
The lightless world has compensating qualities.
Through thermal currents I sense
Variations in the darkness
It isn't just a monotone deep black.
The browns are warm
The grays less tepid
The blues and greens
Have hints of coolness.

I feel submerged in waters of
A tropic sea at dusk, slithering in depths
Within a deep kaleidoscope
Of changing blues and greens
So soothing, so relaxing, so hypnotic.

There is a timelessness within
This world without addresses,
With neither maps, nor clear co-ordinates
Without a sun, without a moon, or stars
With nothing to remind me
Of whom, of where, of when or why.
I feel oblivion to the nth degree
In depths of nonchalance unlimited!

This is an enigmatic episode,
An interlude of sleep that simulates
The strange nirvana of death upon the living.

Strangely, I do not wake up ecstatic after this.
I often feel that I was cheated by the blankness of the night
And have the nerve to curse sleep for being a waste,
Because I have forgotten the exquisiteness
Of restful, dreamless sleep.

Of Sleep and Death

Sleep and death are not the same
Despite the similes and metaphors
Including mine, that leap across
The abyss between them.

Death is a scabrous, ugly subject
That often comes through dreadful agonies
And makes us beg for blandishments.
Avoid: "he died." Say: "passed away."
"He joined the Lord; he rests in Heaven."

Such palliatives don't work for me
I don't believe in Heaven or in hell
I only see eternal nothingness in death.

But here's the difference.
While death is bleak, arcane
Macabre, everlasting,
Especially as it looms ahead of us,
Sleep is rich, and brief, recurrent
Rejuvenating and mysterious.

Sleep is wondrous even when
It mimics death in dreamless interludes
When we're deprived of all our senses
And Death appears nonthreatening and natural
Because we catch it in our rearview mirror
Just as it was before we ever were.

Don't you remember?
It was when life existed for others, but not us
When we were yet unborn
When nonexistence was neither sad nor sinister
But like a dreamless sleep
From which we awoke.

The Transnighter

Awake for over twenty hours,
I am from Planet Yesterday
Trespassing on Today
While tethered to the past
And stretching to the limit
My leash on wakefulness.

For me, Time runs amok
The clocks appear as soft
And molten metal in Dali paintings.
My bearings lost, I now confuse
Sunrises with sunsets
My breakfasts with my suppers
Mis-flavored by the warp of time.

So many things are wrong.
The morning air is much too fresh for me
I long to breathe the warm
Recycled mellow air
Of my own breath upon my pillow.

I'm a shipwrecked time traveler
Marooned in a forbidden day
A fish out of water gasping for
The sea of sleep.
A lone hitchhiker on a road

Unseen by passing cars
I'm thumbing for a car that will not come
I'm thumbing for a bed to take me home.

Drowsiness

The senses ebb, alertness drops
And motivation wanes as torpor creeps
And eyelids turn to leaded curtains.

The body clamors for sleep
And grouses at the noisy world
The muscles issue ultimatums
Threatening work stoppages
Ignoring orders to be alert.

The brain refuses to do arithmetic,
And goes AWOL, stealing seconds of oblivion
In golden little snoozes.
Now neither food nor drink tempt anymore
And sex is an annoyance.

An insatiable yearning for rest
Makes Death a consummation
Devoutly to be wished
If only it could be had in finite quantities.

Insomnia

My bed, a rudderless ship
And I, its helpless passenger.
I'm living in a storm of sleep denial
Turning, tossing, pushing buttons and levers
In control panels without power.

I mimic a catatonic state
And count imaginary sheep
But all I manage is to dawdle
In stillness without rest,
In darkness without calm
In silence without peace.

The night could be a peaceful grave
For those entombed in restful sleep,
But it buries me alive. In my despair
I hear a ghastly noise, a hemorrhage of time.
It is the sound of life
That gushes minutes into hours, all going to the gutter.

What would I give for only a little whiff,
For just a tiny little sniff
From the vial of death?
Just a half a drop to sip
For a night's worth of sleep.

2

SLEEP: THE LOST THIRD OF OUR LIVES

Accounting for Sleep

We need sleep.
Good health demands it
And nature must obey necessity.
But then, how much is optimal?
It seems a third of every day,
About eight hours, is average.

On daily terms, a third
Each day seems fine
And causes no dismay.

The trouble is that over 60 years
This rate accumulates
To 20 years of sleep.
And this, we'd all agree,
Does cause distress.

What do we have to show
For all these years of sleep?
It is this gaping void
That gave the title to this book
The lost third of our lives.

This is the glaring waste that sends
Us on a quest to find redeeming value.
We dreamed, didn't we?
Do dreams not count?
Ah yes, indeed. We dream.
That cannot be denied.
But dreams can't fill the void
If they can't be recalled.

You could have lived
In Shangri-La for twenty years
But if you can't remember them
Those years are lost and have no value.
It is the size of so much life
Evaporated like a puff
That seems unconscionable
And unforgivable.
You can't help feeling cheated.
You can't accept the waste.

And so, you embark upon a quest
To find the hidden treasures of the night
And raid oblivion's caves
To find the lost third of your life.

Z z z Z

Do Unremembered Dreams Have Value?

But just because you can't recall your dreams
Does not establish that they didn't occur
Or that they had no value.

What if you enjoyed them while they lasted?
Does that not count?
A once-in-a-lifetime meal
A banquet at a royal castle
Has value even if
You cannot name the things you had.

And what if you received a magic gift
During your unremembered dream?
A gift that kept on giving inexplicably
A gift that only Heaven can bestow.

It could have happened in a night
When you were still a child.
A beautiful lady, a Muse,
Approached your bed
Syringe in hand and then
Injected in your arm a magic potion
That gave you a special talent
A gift that helped materialize
All the successes of your future life.
It could have been a great affinity for art
For science, politics, athletics, dance, or music.

You awoke possessing a sharp eye,
An ear with perfect pitch,
A nose, a touch, a golden voice
That served you well through life.
You stored it, not in memory,
But in the sinews of your heart.

The magic potion lit a fire
Becoming a lodestar
That shone from embers of
An unremembered dream
That opened doors for you.

For Martin Luther King Jr.
It was the glow he saw
Above a mountain top
The altar of freedom where he
Would lead his people.

For JFK it was the audacity to
To put an American on the moon
Before the end of the decade
And bring him safely home.
This at a time when we were far behind
The Soviets in space.

Some unremembered dreams
May be encounters with the Gods
With inexplicable mysterious forces
That then evolved to make us who we are.

Z z z z

Remembered Dreams

But dreams that we recall
Besides being rare
Are also brief.
They last for only minutes
And typically occur
Just as we awake.

They are the fading remnants
That conscious memory
Can snatch from sleep and drag
Across the liminal edge
The threshold of yesterday and today.

What of the other dreams
We might have had much earlier
In the cocoon of our wee hours?
Those dreams are gone and lost forever.

Our sleeping memory possesses
A short recording tape
Which tapes over itself
Erasing everything before.

We can't record and save
Our dreams for later viewing.
The dreams concocted in the deep of night
Will come and go as if they never were.
Unless, of course, you wake up suddenly at 3 am
And snatch the dream's tail end.

Awakening is always violent.
It shatters the brittle crystal of a dream
It tears the dreaming stage
Which cannot stand
The world of open eyes, the onslaught
Of world awareness that comes
In overwhelming avalanches
To blanch the dream away.

The most that we can do
Is grasp the tail-end of a dream
Which is at most
About four minutes long.
If the dream was impactful
Engaging and absorbing
Its scenes can play throughout the day
In tantalizing images that could endure.

The fleeting visions of that dream
Might leave you with a haunting question
A question that will take you years to answer.
A question such as: who am I?
As in the next two inscrutable dreams.

z   z   z   z   Z

Inner Echoes of a Poetess in a Mathematician's Body

I am the voice that whispers
In the womb of your subconscious
The fantasies that you dismiss as silly.

So near and yet so far apart we are
So intimate, and yet almost strangers
While living in one body.

We meet during sleep, not touching
Moving shadows on the screen of dreams,
Silhouettes eclipsing past each other.

Strands of one psyche
We're similar, but not identical
Each with her own proclivities.

You, the mathy one, teaching by day
And using up the hours of our mind
On job, on duty and on banausic chores.

While I wait all day for the night,
For the depth of sleep to emerge in dreams
To speak of love and poetry.

You wish to see me? Stand before a mirror
And look into your eyes. I'm waving
From the depth of your pupils.

Self-Reflections in Dreams

Deep in a dream, she sees a mirror on the wall
Its liquid darkness aglitter with moonbeams
Mysteriously whispering her name.

A breeze blows by pressing her nightgown
Against her body, draping and sculpting
Her feminine anatomy.

She wonders if the mirror is what it appears to be:
A dark and shiny liquid on the wall.
Was she to touch it, would it feel wet?

She gets the nerve to touch it, and suddenly
Its surface curves around her like a billowing wave
That then embraces her and swallows her.

"I got you," it says.
"Now you are me.
Feel what I feel, see what I see!"

From her cold and crystal prison
She sees the room where she had stood before
Unchanged. And yet, it is a foregone world.

She's now a siren in a depth of darkness
Reflecting images to those who approach her
To let them see themselves.

Ah, here comes my first customer
A woman, young like me
My height and body build.

She dances in the moonlight
A peacock bolted from
Her cage of inhibitions.

The lass is hauntingly familiar
The siren wonders if she knows her
If she is... if she could be...

Oh, yes, oh yes, she is
She's me!
She is my clone!

Except, except, she's so at ease
So confident, so assured
No shy stutterer like me!

Oh, look at her! Such panache!
So eloquent with body language
She dares express what I repress.

Goodness, she's carrying lingerie to model
Skimpy, stringy rags I do not like
And would not wear.

She is peeling off her clothes.
Where is this going? Should I not watch?
I must admit, the strings become her.

A thousand questions I would ask her
If only I could, like who, just who?
Just who are you?

Are you the apparition of what I want to be,
If only I had the nerve?
Or are you, perhaps, the inner me I fear to be?

z Z Z Z z

Art in Dreams and Dreams as Art

I

Some works of art take years
Of tedious crafting to complete,
A dream but minutes and no more.
A dream is unrehearsed creation
That blossoms on the go
Without recourse to tweak, to age, or gel.

And yet, for all its rapid execution
For all its helter-skelter evolution,
A dream at times imbues sensations
Which justify comparison with art.

A dream is but a puff of memory
Intangible, non-marketable
And non-negotiable.
As such, it's free to plagiarize
To reproduce real works of art
Behind our shuttered eyes
That show Van Gogh at work on Starry Night
While Debussy is playing Claire de Lune
 And all for the price of a snore!

And while a dream exhausts its light
In minutes of a single night
It's also true that sleeping time
Enjoys a magical fluidity
That stretches minutes into hours

Prolonging the precious seconds of a kiss
To endless bliss.
The magic clockwork of our dreams
Makes things be more than what they seem.

The language of our dreams is often virtual
Conveyed by silent telepathic words
In rhymed profundities
That riddle and perplex our thinking mind
But titillate the heart's illogic mind.

It is in dreams that our spirit rises from its weary body,
And we become a ghost, a spectral somebody.
We're ageless in temporal space
Unbound in cosmic space.
We navigate in ways we couldn't imagine while awake
And live sojourns in times we'd never know awake.

But dreams can also take us to the depths of hell
Entrapping us in nightmares with eerie spells
That scare us off our wits.
And yet, we manage to survive.
For dreams have ways to bring us out alive.
If nothing else, a deus ex machina comes up
To take us safely over the top.
We find ourselves awake in bed
And ready for the day ahead.

II

But enough now. No more abstractions and descriptions.
Here is a dream I'll share with you.
I was up high above the clouds, distraught
And feeling like a kitten up a tree.
At nearly twenty thousand feet above the ground
Upon a ladder between two mountain peaks
That were some hundred miles apart.
The sun was to my right, a rising ball of fire
That warmed the chilly sky and gave its luster to
The clouds and land below.
Aha, I thought, the morning sun being East

This ladder goes from north to south,
The same direction as the Ecuadorian Andes
A cordillera of volcanoes and snow-capped mountains
That I had seen it from an airline window once before.
Its majesty was so imposing and so beautiful!
The wind blew through the canyons and brought
The plaintive sounds of Andean airs, of pieces like *Alturas,
El Condor Pasa* and *La Partida* with their distinctive instruments:
Charangos, quenas, and zampoñas. So sweet and melancholy.
Up north, ahead of me, I recognized Mt Cotopaxi
And to the south the Chimborazo loomed even larger.
It seemed quite likely that my ladder was anchored to those peaks.
But how and why was I there? And what should I do now?
The distance to the Cotopaxi seemed shorter.
So, reaching it became my one and only plan
To touch the solid ground again.

III

I don't like heights. And least of all, precarious heights.
How strange that I had not freaked out.
But dreams can furnish us
The compensating antidotes to adversity.
I also didn't feel cold, nor thirst, nor hunger.
My only torment was the loneliness
The excruciating pangs of solitude from being
Marooned so high, exiled,
Rejected by the world.

Just then my antidote for solitude
Came crashing on my ladder.
It almost knocked me off.
I nearly died of fright. What was that?
It was too big to be a buzzard,
Perhaps a condor?
The jolt was so strong that it dislodged my ladder from
Its Cotopaxi moorings.
I could not see a mountain at its northern end anymore.
Who knows where else I was now headed to?

IV

I couldn't believe my luck.
My solitary dream had sent me quite a compensating grace.
The intrusive object was no buzzard but an angel!
A princess, a lovely creature, a beautiful young woman
Who had been sent to keep me company in high hell.
How beautiful she was! I was in heaven now.
I could exist with her like this,
Forever.
She was Asiatic, most likely Japanese.
"Ah, welcome!" I said: "You are the answer to my prayers."
But she didn't understand and flashed a gracious smile.
I would have said much more, if only I knew her language,
If only she spoke mine.
Communication will be a problem, I thought.
But not insuperable and it would not
Diminish one iota the joy I felt
To have her company.
I could just gaze contentedly at her
And do charades with her for decades.
I gazed at her, examining her features,
As people stare at works of art and dote on Mona Lisa.
She was a living work of art. Enthralling, mesmerizing.

V

I wanted to know volumes about her.
How does she sound? What does she think?
How does she feel about things, about the world, about me?
I thought of ways to probe her thoughts, her voice, her feelings.
And language or no language, I started.
I pointed to Mt Chimborazo to our south.
It loomed so large that it was daunting.
Then softly I said: "Mt Chimborazo."
As if on cue, the clouds aligned themselves below its icecap,
And formed the letters that spelled its name.
She read them slowly: "Chim-bo-ra-zo."
I heard her voice at last. What music! What joy!
She had a quaint and charming accent.
And then I asked her if she knew where
This ladder went because the Cotopaxi

No longer seemed aligned with us.
She read my mind and pointed to the far
Indefinite northwest and said: "Fuji-San."
By some bewitchment, a faint reflection of Mt Fuji
Showed up in the upper stratosphere.
We were talking. We were communicating.
We could orient ourselves. And we could learn from each other.
We had a long, long way to go. But we had time galore.
And we had started.

      VI

The next idea to explore was names.
I knew a few Japanese girl names.
They fascinated me for being so cute and pretty.
Would she be Cio-Cio-San? As in Puccini's Butterfly?
But that would be too coincidental.
There was *Himari*, sunflower;
Ichika, love fragrance; *Mizuki*, felicitous omen, hope.
Izumi, fountain, spring; *Kimiko*, beautiful child.
Misake, beautiful blossom.
I once read that the syllables hi, ma, ki, mi, ko, zu
Embody ideas which, when put together create a composite word
Whose various sources add tinges to the name.
Should I just rattle off these names and see which hit?
I opted for a more direct approach.
I pointed to myself and said: "Eduardo."
She understood and called my name.
It was such music to my ears.
Then she released one hand from the ladder
And pointing at herself, she said: "Mizuki."
We had identified ourselves.

      VII

Our silent moments were not empty.
I played music in my mind which, thanks to the
Phenomenon "only-in-dreams," she also heard.
The music came as if an orchestra of a thousand angels
Were playing, reverberating in the heavens.

It was eclectic, varied, mostly classical.
The first to emerge was Khatchaturian's Adagio from Spartacus.
Its melody is a boa constrictor that slithers around
The sinews of my heart and squeezes my soul every time.
It wasn't all symphonic. At times, it was pianistic as in
Prokofiev's Vision Fugitives and the Moderato from his Four Etudes.
At times it was vocal as in the Aria from Bachianas Brasileiras No. 5
Of Heitor Villa-Lobos. And then we came to
The languorous strains of the second movement
Of Mozart's piano concerto Number 21. Its sweet
Ethereal notes suffused the air embracing us,
Intoxicating us with deep ineffable sensations that could
Be summarized with but a single word: love.
To my delight she knew the music and had
Identified each one of the composers I had played.
Shakespeare had it right.
The marriage of true minds
Does not admit impediments.
We hardly spoke. There were no words between us,
Just touches and soft rubs, caresses.

VIII

Our ladder had become a bed to us, a nest, our aerie.
It was about three feet wide and thousands of miles long.
Sometimes we sat upon its rungs facing each other.
Sometimes we lay across the rungs and curled our arms and legs
In loops around some rungs to make us more secure and took a nap.
By now we had decided that Mt Chimborazo,
And certainly Mt Fuji, were impossible goals.
We'd never get to either one. Deep down, our hearts didn't want to.
Deep down, we wanted to stay put,
To settle down upon our ladder and create
A brave new world upon the heavens.
We'd be like Adam and Eve, as it were,
Progenitors of an airborne human species that lived
Upon a latticework of ladders that crisscrossed the sky.
But ah, how presumptuous of me! We hadn't even kissed yet.
How would we procreate while hanging on to keep from falling?
Could dreams be that accommodating?
Somehow, I thought we'd find a way. We'd figure it out.

I even pictured possibilities.

IX

"Mizuki, I love you," I began, not audibly, osmosis like, as through
Telepathy, the language medium of most dreams.
She knew my thoughts implicitly. And so,
Without further ado, our lips entwined, and we had our first kiss.
And then a second, a third and countless others.
I touched her breasts. She didn't object and helped,
Unbuttoning her blouse, revealing
Two miniature replicas of Mts Fuji and Chimborazo on her chest.
So conical, so irresistible! I kissed them both,
And sucked their summits.
I felt I was a God, a Jupiter no less,
About to ravish Mother Earth.
We hugged and held each other tight.
And then the heavens rattled. Our ladder shook.
It wasn't what you'd think.
It was a salvo of lightnings that hit our ladder
And tore our aerie apart.
It was the deus ex machinas that finally
Had come to rescue me, but at the most inopportune time.
The ladder came undone. The rungs went flying everywhere.
I saw Mizuki one last time as she went flying out of sight.
I plummeted, free-falling to the ground which grew bigger
And bigger by the second.
Oh God, here comes the big splash. Goodbye world.
But strangely, it never came.
Instead, I started feeling lighter,
As if I were a feather lazily wafting to and fro
Before alighting gently on my bed.

X (Epilogue)

When all the props of fantasy collapsed
When all the magic ended, and the dream imploded
When all the luster of the sun upon the world began to fade
And all the quenas and zampoñas quieted
I still could see the fading scenes of paradise
Reprising in my memory,

But they were vanishing fast.
My dream was dying.
It was like seeing the Mona Lisa burning.
Awakening dispels a dream
As fire devours a work of art.
If any scenes remain unburned,
Forgetting comes to mop them up.
The kiss of death first comes
When conscience, a puritanical art critic,
Declares the dream to be a dirty little secret.
It then unleashes rationality and morality,
With all their myriad tentacles,
To have at it and strangle it.
Before I knew it, I was extricating myself from the dream.
Denying any involvement.
No, no, I did not conjure up that dream.
It wasn't me!
It was an elf within my brain who made of me
A young and spectral somebody
A lad who didn't fear heights
And had the nerve to use my body and name.
It wasn't me.
I'm just an old, old man who's terrified of heights,
Who's old enough to be his great grandfather,
Who is long, long married, and happily to boot.
And so, be gone hallucinations!
The real world is calling.
I have no time for ladders in the sky.
Goodbye you too, my lovely gentle geisha,
Whatever your name was.

Daydreams

It's axiomatic that dreams
Cannot be extended once we awake.
For once our consciousness intrudes
The dream is gone forever.
We could remain in bed
And we could even dream again
But it will be a different dream.

For dreams are whimsy
Free-spirited imaginings
That hate the meddling of
Controlling critical thinking.

When you go back to sleep to extend a dream
You're no longer drifting with the dream
You are driving it. You are cheating.
You are daydreaming.

While dreams are random disconnected tales,
Daydreams are manipulated contrivances.
At times they are so long and so elaborate
That they become immortal works of fiction.

If we could lengthen dreams
Concatenating them in series
If we resumed tonight
Where we left off last night
Our dreams would be continuous

And would have histories that filled
The void of our existence.
We'd have a diurnal and nocturnal life
A parallel existence in a dual world
There'd be no waste in all those years we slept.

Z Z   z   Z Z

Sleep's Mysterious Memory

Why, if we sleep for hours
Do we remember only
Just minutes of our dreams?
It seems that dreams are made
Within the blackhole of our minds
From which no dreams escape.

I'm told we have two memories
Which are completely separate
And independent of each other.
One is *sleep-memory*. Brief, short-lived.
The other is *conscious-memory*.
Enduring and augmentable. Elastic.

Sleep memory is mysterious
Inscrutable, arcane and niggardly.
Its dreams are stingily curtailed as if
They were recorded with a video tape so short
It holds at most four minutes worth of dreams.
For longer dreams, the tape starts rewinding
Erasing previous dreams.
You couldn't wake up at 8 a.m.
And summon what you dreamt at 3 a.m. because
By then the dream would have been copied over many times.

If we cannot remember what we dreamt just hours ago
Imagine the futility of summoning the dreams we had
A week, a month or year ago.

The only way to save our dreams
Is by transcribing them to a permanent medium
A diary, a tape recorder
The instant that we awake.

Most people don't do that
And so, our dreams,
Are doomed to be forgotten.

By contrast, *conscious memory* is generous
Efficient, expandable, reliable, and enduring.
It loves the view from open eyes
And thrives in brightness, absorbing and retaining
New knowledge and ideas through decades
From kindergarten to the PhD and then beyond.
It graciously expands to accommodate
Ambitious scholars with a second PhD
And fluency in various foreign tongues.

Not so *Sleep memory* which works strictly during sleep
Each night being independent and unrelated
To previous sleep sessions.
We can't hoard dreams.
Our dreams are tethered with a leash so short
They never roam beyond sleep-memory's realm
But if they try, they'll hit a wall of mist
That rises from a moat around her kingdom
Converting escaping dreams to fog.

Don't blame our long-term memory
For having meager dream archives.
That is the most it could steal
From niggardly sleep memory.

Z Z z z

Stealing Dreams

I've tried in many ways to steal my dreams
To no avail.
I've had a pad of paper and a pen beside my bed.
One night I even had a tape recorder.
The Goddess of Sleep discovered me red-handed.
She took my writing pad and said:

"Oh, silly man, don't you know
Our ink becomes invisible
The moment you wake up?
Besides, there is no need to steal.
You may scoop away
Whatever dreams you want.
But you will need a ladle for that
Which I'll provide for you.
So, choose the dreams you want
While I go get the ladle."

With all those hours of dreams available to me
And with the right to all of them
I was a child jailed in a candy store.

Then she returned
And brought her magic ladle.
It was slightly bigger than a thimble!
It scooped just minutes-worth of dreams
And nothing more.

I woke up taunted by a mocking laughter
The ladle was such a tasteless joke
Was I supposed to thank her for it?

She plays such tricks on us. But why?
Why use a videotape so limited?
Why bother with a leash so short?
Why make the ink invisible?
Why give me a ladle so small?
And why the moat that turns our dreams to fog?
All signs suggest *sleep-memory* is
A kingdom of darkness
That guards its world
With iron hand and doesn't share
Its treasures...why?

Because we were not meant
To sleep our life away
Nor love our dreams too much.
A dozen things in life are more important than sleep,
Survival being the first.

We are equipped to face
The challenges of life
And stay alive
With two thirds of each day
For wakefulness
And only a third for sleep.

The real world –and not the bed
Is meant to be our great arena
Our place of work,
The battleground of our struggle
The ground on which we must survive
And leave our legacy.

If sleep is necessary, survival is more so.
In life-and-death situations
Survival always trumps sleep.
There's no timeout for sleep in war.
We manage sleep in shifts
While sentinels keep watch.

And then there's this:
Sleep provides us with a sense of kinesthesia
A *proprioception* also known as a sixth sense

THE LOST THIRD OF OUR LIVES

In which our nervous system is in sync with
Our muscular system.
Both work during sleep imbuing us with
An awareness that keeps us
From falling out of bed.
But tots and babies do not have it yet
So, cradles must be enclosed
To keep them safe.

Asleep we are useless
We're unproductive to the world
Like kittens, babies, senile folk.

Awake we're active,
Discharging our responsibilities
Contributing, creating
Performing all the myriad things that life requires.

We're in this world to make the most of life
And we can do so only while awake
When we can work and can create

The deeds that will define us
So that our life awake becomes
The envy of dreams.
This is the grand design.

Z z z z z

Sleep's Magic

The brain, a tireless workaholic, never stops
Not even during sleep
When eyes are closed and we're
Immersed in interludes of simulated coma
It goes about through peace and quiet
Performing tasks, uninterrupted by distractions.

Some tasks are physiological and biochemical
Ensuring body parts get their juices
Recycling cells
Resuscitating weary body parts
Replenishing depleted energy
Reconstituting aged anatomy
Rejuvenating it for yet another day.

These tasks alone give proof that sleep
Couldn't possibly be the waste
That it appears to be.
But there is more.
There's also magic.

Some days we go to bed exhausted and bedraggled
Retreating from the war zone of the working world.
We're full of uncompleted tasks.
The bed is our salvation, a mother's arms
A refuge from our sea of troubles.
We plump in bed and tuck our woes

Beneath our pillow and fall asleep.
We quit the battle for that day.

Incredibly, the blessed brain takes up for us.
It studies our situation and thinks it through.
It weighs our options for tomorrow
Consulting its diverse compartments
In chats that we're not privy to.

We rise next morning unaware
Of what our brain discussed
But feeling stronger, wiser.
And bubbling with resolve
To try again what we gave up for lost.

Somehow, we know what we must do.
Something happened during sleep
That found the answer to our riddles
And magically solved our problems.

The brain took up our problems while we slept
Retracing our steps, revisiting the scenes.
Sometimes it was a key we lost,
A document misplaced,
A crossword puzzle we couldn't solve
A theorem, an algorithm gone afoul
A tricky and complex set of options
We couldn't choose from.

We wasted hours in vain the day before
And fell asleep convinced we lost the battle
But when we awoke, we learned to our surprise,
That we had won the war.

Our brain produced a wonderful surprise:
It served in bed a breakfast platter
With all our problems solved.
Projected on our mind's screen there was
A throbbing X that marked the spot
Where we could find the misplaced object.
Or we awoke to a dawning in our mind

A rising sun of understanding that brought
The bright epiphany of an Eureka moment
With the solution to our math problem
The missing link to the algorithm
The critical clue to the word-puzzle
The optimal decision to select.

Cerebral magic such as this is real.
It has been documented by numerous
Anecdotal accounts and by the scientific literature.
The brain would be the first to downplay it all
By saying, as geniuses will do,
It isn't magic…just doing its job.

We attribute it to a miracle
And thank our lucky stars.
We hardly ever laud
The brain and its sleeping minions
Except when inadvertently we say:
"I'll sleep on it."

Z Z z Z Z

Dream-Making

More so than dreams themselves
Dream-making has intrigued mankind forever.
Oneiromancers, soothsayers and psychiatrists
Have tried to understand it.

Who makes the dreams and why?
How are the topics chosen?
Are dreams a message?
From whom to whom?
How do they come about?

And though the scientists now know
That rapid eye movement is a sign of dreaming
And though they trace electric charges
And see the flows of blood
From zone to zone and lobe to lobe
They have not ever seen the dream themselves
And never will.

Our dreams and their making
Remain a secret only dreamers see.
But we can all opine
And here's my view.

Some time while deep in sleep
The dark, plutonian world
Of our *subconscious* comes alive.
Arcane and distant, it's like
The outer fringes of the solar system

Except it isn't up, but down
It isn't far, but near, so close
It is within us.

It's like an inner theater
A Hollywood studio in the brain
Accessible exclusively through sleep
And it is magical, fantastical, bewildering.

The imagination is let loose and runs
Full throttle to its highest power.
The laws of physics are suspended and upended.
The notion of the impossible is voided.
We travel faster than the speed of light
And reach the edges of the Milky Way
Traversing at the speed of thought.
You think it, you're there, regardless of the distance.
We flit from future to the past
We go through walls, we walk on water
We slither through the flames of hell unburned.

To this enchanted world now comes
A caravan of creatures
The actors of our dreams who want to know
What role they'll play tonight.

It is a motley crew that represents
The disassembled parts of self
The nuts and bolts of our own psyche.
We frequently refer to them
By their collective words:
The soul, the psyche, the self, our inner being.
But that would not apply this time
Since they have turned their singularity to a plurality,
To defragmented elements of our persona
And they have taken human form.

Assembled are your ego, alter egos, oracles
Libido, muses and even conscience
Who, by the way, appears accompanied by Guilt,
Her mean sidekick, that's poised to extract
Remorse out of your bones.

We never see these creatures when awake.
We're only vaguely aware of them by day.
As puppets on their strings, we feel
The lift and pull upon our limbs
We hear the angel standing on our shoulder
That whispers good advice upon one ear
While Satan on the other shoulder
Is pitching his nefarious spiel.

This is a fractious bunch that speaks
With many voices and is too intractable
To finish a sensible coherent dream all on its own.
Someone on high must intervene to impose
Control and discipline.

And so, the brain becomes a playwright, showman
Director and producer of our sleep productions
And turns the creatures into thespians.

The brain must keep in line the prima donnas
Who have their own ideas about their roles
And vie to have their moment on the spotlight
And clamor for a major role.
Each one would be a star.

Some actors crave control beyond the theater
They're past controlling only dreams
They would control your life itself, your destiny.
They would remold you to their heart's content.

Libido, a reincarnation of Eve,
Is beautiful
She struts around
A carnal embodiment of sin itself
Aloof and irrepressible.
If she could have her way
We'd have X-rated dreams night after night.
Her push and pull is raw and strong.

The brain tries keeping her on a short leash
And watches constantly over her
Insisting that she observe good taste
And keep things decent.
But that is a continual fight night after night.

Somehow, the brain prevails and brings
Teamwork and order to our dreams.
Committees are created and they decide
The subject of the dream
And who will play what roles.

Quite often conscience has her way
She has an axe to grind
She has priority over morality
She has a lot of clout politically
And has a lot of say on dreams.

Z z Z z Z

Encounters with Conscience

Most dreams are fluff and chaff
Cartoonish, childish plays
That we will readily forget.
Not so the episodes with conscience
Which are of transcendental consequence
Which teach you lessons that
Are apt to change your life.

She will accost you during sleep
To bring you your comeuppance.
Remember when you binged on malice?
She tried to stop you, to make you reconsider
But she had little sway with you
Because you were awake
And you could shut her up.

And so, she waited patiently and ground her axe
And waited for the night when she could catch you sleep
And then unload on all the accumulated sins.

She then re-played the nasty scenes
And made you feel the hurt your victims felt.
You felt the wheels of justice rolling over you,
She threw you in the washer
She squeezed you through the wringer
She tumble-dried you clean

You felt denuded, cooked alive,
Exposed for what you are.

Unfortunately, some people
Have thick skins
Remorse has no effect
On rotten souls.

Poor conscience can't control them
Or turn them into better human beings.
These perps succeed in getting conscience off their backs
And once they've gotten rid of her,
Without her aegis and her compass,
They turn satanic, mean, despicable.

One of these rotten punks
Was sitting on death row one day
And as he took stock of his evil life
He wondered how it was
That he became so bad.

He couldn't recall the night
When in an unremembered dream
He strangled conscience with his
Bare hands and shot her mascot,
A Doberman as mean as he.

The following day he felt emancipated
Unbridled by the mores of right and wrong
And free to lie, to rob and rape
He killed in wanton rage
And never felt remorse.

z z Z z z

Games Conscience Plays

I've called Conscience
A virago, a nasty pesky shrew.
But that was over 70 years ago
When I was still a teen that knew it all.
I've mellowed now
And conscience doesn't nag me anymore
She feels as comfy as well-worn shoes.

And yet, from time to time she still surprises me
With odd nightmares where she
Will conjure up situations I do not recognize
And make me wallow in recrimination
With pangs of shame for sins I didn't commit.

The columnist Marilyn vos Savant once published
A letter from a reader who wondered if she was
The only one who had recurring dreams with common theme.
She dreamt she was in school and hadn't been to class in weeks.

This dream recurred every few months or so
She was consumed by guilt and was unable to explain
How that had come about. She never did that in real life.
She felt ashamed, completely helpless.
And then she was stunned to learn
That readers by the hundreds
Responded saying they also had the same nightmare.

I too have had variations of this dream
As student and professor.
There's method to the madness.
How else would people know

Of sins they haven't yet committed?
How would Mother Teresa know
Of drunkenness and its hangover?

This is the after-hours university
Conveying heuristic lessons
About what's right and proper

You shouldn't be late
You shouldn't cut classes
You shouldn't be irresponsible.

In just one dream you learn at once
The sin, its guilt, and its remorse.

If you are not guilty of this sin
Forget the intrusion
It's no big deal
You have no permanent scars
Wake up and feel absolved.
You might be a little wiser.

Z Z z z z

Can We See Conscience While Awake?

In dreams she appears in various forms.
At times female, at times a man
She borrows images of others
Appearing often as a person we respect
An icon from the past
A hero from our day.
The young will often see her as
A parent, teacher, preacher, or a cop.

Seeing conscience while awake
Is even easier than in dreams.
But just be warned,
You may not like what you will see.
She's known to be brutally honest
And wouldn't accommodate you with a lie
If you beseeched and begged for one.

She'll say:
"You want to see me? Then stand before a mirror.
I'm there, looking at you."
And you respond: "Yes, but I only see myself."
And she retorts: "What did you expect?
We share the same anatomy, you know."
And then she adds:
"For days I have been telling you
To watch your diet and every time

You shushed me up by stuffing cupcakes
In our mouths. Now look at you.
You're hideously overweight."

That cured your curiosity of seeing conscience.
You got sick at the stomach from the sight.
You run away aghast, disgusted with yourself
And cursed the mirror.

In dreams she tends to be much kinder.
She has appeared to me as Janet Reno
Attorney General of the United States.
One time she was Mother Theresa
And many times, she took the form
Of Lincoln, my most venerable oracle.
That was a treat.

Sometimes in dreams she'll be
More mollifying, kinder.
She'll be a rabbi, priest, or preacher.
She'll accentuate your better traits.

She might appear as Martin Luther King, Jr.
And say in a mellifluous voice:
"You are what you are physically
 And there is little you can do
About your stature, weight, or race.
Don't bother about that.
Present your worthier attributes
Which fair-minded people will appreciate.
They will not judge you by

The color of your skin or by the way you look
But by the content of your character."
You'll feel absolved. You'll want to celebrate
And so, you have another cupcake.

Z Z z z Z

Oracles and Prophecy

Today we can access the mind of intellectuals
Of pundits, columnists, professionals
Through TV, radio, through the web and printed media.
For those who need them, there are Dear Abby and such.
Our oracles include people we've admired
From Jesus Christ to Lincoln
From preachers, teachers and mentors we respect.
We have the record of their thoughts
Which is archived in conscious memory
And which we're able to access during sleep.
A cameo appearance of these oracles
Suffices to imbue authority to your sleeping thoughts.

In Roman times they did not have
As many sources as we do
But they had oracles enough.
The very word derives from there.

The story goes Calpurnia dreamt the death
Of Julius Caesar the night before the ides of March.
And many people think it was clairvoyance.
Do dreams foretell the future?
I have another take on that.

I think Calpurnia knew the Roman Senators
And read the waves that emanated from their hearts
She sniffed their sweat and caught the smell of blood.

She did not trust them.
She went to bed that night besieged with fears
Assailed by worries, in despair.

And while she slept, she invoked her oracles
The people she trusted and respected
Who mulled her case and understood her fears.
They thought she was right on.
Her premonitions were eminently rational.

To show support her oracles expressed
Agreement with her fears
And staged their vision of tomorrow
In one nightmare that showed
What would befall to Julius Caesar if he
Was present at the Senate the next day.

The oracles knew the senators well.
They knew their fears, their greed
Their Machiavellian machinations.
It was a cabal so predictable, so obvious.

With gore galore, with silver streaks
Of knives that cut the air
Calpurnia saw how Caesar's blood oozed out
And stained his white and limpid toga.

The assassination was history foretold.
Calpurnia tried to keep him home
But in her heart, she knew the Ides of March
Was carved on his tombstone.

ZZ z ZZ

Muses

These are the goddesses that light
A flame of inspiration which will
Endure until your dying day.
These are the stars that guide
Your path through life.

And yet, you can't remember
The transcendental day
They came into your life.
It was so long ago
That you were only a child.
In Mozart's case, he wasn't even five.

They set up court within your brain
Within your heart enabling you to
Excel in various fields
That turn you into a star
An idol, an envy of the world.

They bring to you creative verve
The passion for a cause
The vision of artistic structures
Ideas that will change the world
And herald a new age.

They'll make of you an icon of your time
Conferring brilliance, talent, creativity
And urging you to keep the flame alive
To nurture it and make the best
Of all the gifts you've been conferred
To ensure your place in history.

Hans Christian Anderson, the Brothers Grimm
Walt Disney all of them were visited by muses.
But also Thomas Edison, and Martin Luther King
Da Vinci, Einstein and John Fitzgerald Kennedy.

There was no single dream
That brought the transformation
At least not one they could recall.
There was no dialogue because
They talked in telepathic tones
Soliloquies instead of dialogue
As I talking to Me.

The muses are invisible spirits
Within the artist's psyche
That speak to him through atoms in the air
There are no records for their encounters
What I relate herein is fiction.

It could have taken place
In one of those forgotten sessions
In the depth of the wee hours
When blossoms burgeoned in the dark
Of unremembered dreams.

And yet they were the source
Of visions, quests and life-long missions.
There is no question Martin Luther King
Was driven by a dream.
He said as much.
It's true he didn't provide details
About the where and when
And yet, unarguably he had a dream.

He only knew he was impelled
To lead his people to a distant hill
Through scabrous paths
But in his dream, he saw the mountain top
And he could see his people getting there.

And though he knew his people
Would succeed, he wasn't sure about himself.
There was a premonition that escaped his lips
When he intoned prophetically:
I may not get there with you.

What made him say that?
Was it perhaps the echo of one
Soliloquy recalled in which his muse
Divulged his destiny?

z z Z z z

The Fabulists' Muse

In the case of Hans Christian Andersen
Or the brothers Grimm, J.M. Barrie or Walt Disney
Their Muse may well have come
In fleeting dreams that they prolonged
Till they became an endless reverie,
A daydream that refused to end
And which became one beautiful collection
Of fairy tales and fables that made
Its readers children once again.

It wouldn't surprise me if the muse
Appeared like Tinker Bell herself,
The little pixie flying circles
By Peter Pan and spraying loops
Of fairy dust behind her wake.

"Walt," she said to Disney, "you love fairy tales
And you love drawing.
Have you thought about animating your
Cartoons and turning them to movies?"

And Walt responded: "Yes, I have.
But I dismissed it as impossible."

"Don't be a coward! Of course, it's tedious,
And only one out of a million men could do it
And I feel strongly you're the one.

THE LOST THIRD OF OUR LIVES - 59

The work takes myriad drawings
With similar scenes sequentially
And painstakingly connected
So, when you run them fast tachistoscoptically
They'll capture motion.

"Just think, your characters will have
The gift of motion and expression
Your Donald Duck will have
A waddle in his strut
And, oh, let's not forget,
His voice will have a ducky quack."

Walt was beside himself.
For once he saw it doable
And knew he was the man for it.

At first, his craft was black and white
But that was too mundane.
It did not catch the glory of paradise
His dreams reached higher and higher
For a touch of Heaven here on Earth
And color and music filled the scenes
That followed in *Fantasia, Snow White,
Cinderella, The Lady and the Tramp*.
And many more.

But why stop there?
Why not create the kingdoms
Out of granite and cement
The castles, the costumes and the pageantry?

Why not allow the people to perambulate
The golden lanes and byways of fantastic worlds
In Disneyland and Disneyworld?

Z z Z z Z

Ravel's Muse

He saw her coming, bubbly and cheerful
As sunshine flooding a dark room
And she was bringing news
She had to share or bust.
She came in splendor, as if
Emerging from a bright epiphany
Or bursting from a rainbow.

"Maurice, my love, just brace yourself.
I have just found the challenge you've been waiting for.
There is this Austrian pianist, Paul Wittgenstein,
Who lost his right arm in World War One.
Incredibly, he hasn't given up on music
He's challenging composers, begging them
To write him a piano concerto for the left hand.
He'll pay, of course, for the commission.

"This is so thrilling,
I immediately thought of you.
You're just the man for it.
So please, please tell me you'll do it."

Their conversation went on over several nights,
Ravel but-butting it was forbiddingly difficult.
Yet hearing melodies that swept him off,
Awakening him in the middle of the night

And feeling his left hand had grown to twice its size
And it had grown huge extra fingers.
 Oh yes, he could do it.

He worked indefatigably.
The project which premiered in Paris in 1933
And is a tour de force for two-handed pianists
Who always play it with their left hand.
YouTube has videos by several artists

But the merit of the concerto
Is not the trick and showmanship
Of what a single hand can do.
It's not a dog and pony show.

The merit of the piece is in the music
So beautiful, so perfect
You'd love it even if you did not know
It was a single hand that played
Those glorious finger-hopping arpeggios
Or those glissandos sliding over the keys.
And all the while that hand holds its own
Against an orchestra.

Ravel is in the pantheon of
My favorite composers.
What would I give to have seen
This moment with his muse.

z Z z Z z

JFK: May 21, 1961

He had been President a scant four months
And there he was addressing
Both houses of Congress.
He had assembled them to ask for
An astronomical sum of dollars for a project
That seemed foolhardy.

The Soviets were years ahead of us in space
They had already put satellites
And cosmonauts around the earth
While we were fledglings still.

The very thought of catching up with
The Soviets and beating them to the moon
Was preposterous, undoable
Forbiddingly expensive.

But JFK had the panache and gift of gab
To sell refrigerators to the Eskimos.
His spiel to Congress was well paced
And forcefully delivered.

We would put a man on the moon
And bring him safely home, and
 As if that wasn't enough,
We would accomplish it
Before the end of the decade!

This last stipulation was so bold
That even his Muse choked on it
When she heard a trial run
The night before.

"Oh Jack, you are handsome, brave
Incorrigibly adventurous.
And very, very lucky
But please take out:
Before the end of the decade.
You're promising the impossible."

His Muse was blonde
Didn't look at all like Jacquie O.
But more like Marilyn Monroe.

"What would you give to me
To take it out?"

"Behave now.
I can't give you what you want
And you know it.
That clause is so nervy
No one would take you seriously."

They often bantered like that
They often flirted
He teased, she teased
And still, they got things done.

"I think you're wrong, my pretty!
The clause shows confidence.
The project is so feasible
I can assure delivery
By decade's end.
But we must get started right away.
We can't waste time. That's the point."

The muse was not convinced.
"Don't blame me
Don't say I didn't warn you
If you should fail tomorrow."

Next morning during the speech
She was in the back of the chamber
A bright and huge holograph
That only he could see.

When he came to the end of his spiel
And promised to do it before
The end of the decade
The house broke into thunderous
Heartfelt applause.

The Muse appeared dumbstruck
Agape, muttering: "Well, I'll be…"
He winked at her.

z z Z z z

The Real World in Dreams

Not everything you see in dreams exists
And things that do exist aren't really there
Despite the fact you saw them there.

Dreams are confluences of memories
With flows of wild imagination
Cascading down the slopes of whimsy.

And yet, the real things
The integral parts of sleep such as
The bed, the alarm clock
Don't figure there, hardly ever.
Allow me to correct that.

The Alarm Clock

He's electric these days
And works in silent ways.
His ticking has been muffled
To never again ruffle
His sleepers' calm.

Gone as well
Is his obnoxious bell
Which used to ring
Like a bee sting
In your ears.

Now the digits glow
In a continuous flow
In phosphorescent lines
That morph in pantomimes
Upon a screen.

What's more you can sleep
Quite soundly and deep
Completely free to unwind
With peace of mind
Because he is in charge.

He has a battery pack
Around his back
In order to prevail

In case the power failed
He thinks of everything.

Nor is there any harm
In sleeping past the alarm.
Just press a button on his head
And linger longer in your bed
He'll call you again.

Whatever you do, please
Don't overdo this.
Don't be a glutton
With the snooze button
Or you will press your luck.

He can take once, or twice
But three times is no dice.
He's an ogre by the third buzz
And he'll raise an awful fuss
That you will rue.

He'll shout beyond your ears
Till conscience herself hears
Unleashing a panic attack
That'll bolt you off the sack.
He'll sic guilt on you.

An Ode to the Bed

She is the terminus of battle to which a spent
And weary body turns defeated
In search of rest and refuge at day's end
And she becomes an altar of rebirth
To those she cradles in her bosom
Rejuvenating them to meet another day.

Then she remains unused all day
Forgotten while we're out
And keep our place in sheets
Of white percale and clouds of eiderdown.

She's huge in luxury hotels
Small and humble in log cabins
Imposing in palatial settings
She's raised up on a dais, she's draped
And canopied, adorned with finials
And newels of mahogany
Or filigree of founded brass.

In trendy modern dwellings
She doubles as futons
Convertible divans, or water beds.
In hospitals she's a complex
Synergistic creation
With intricately padded cushions
Of ergonomical correctness

A marvel of engineering design
Mounted over orthopedic mattresses
That pamper our anatomy.

Alas, she can be humble too!
Plain as a hammock, basic as a canvas cot.
Less substantial than a thin tatami mat
As when she's just a cardboard on the floor
Or rumpled sheets of newspaper here and there
Scattered wisps of hay or squalid rags
Strewn over a cold bare ground.
But at its most penurious
She isn't even a skeleton of a bed
She is the ghost of one: a bare dirt floor.

Whatever her form, to burning weary eyes
She is a visage of salvation. A mother's arms!
A safe and cuddling sanctum where you
Can drop all your defenses, entrusting
Your vulnerable hours entirely to her care.

Metaphysically, she transcends her trappings
Becoming a construct of metaphorical dimensions
A launch pad for the spirit's wanderings
A pier for the soul's peregrinations
A port for the flying carpet of our dreams.

More than just a catafalque for sleep
She is the ferry at the service of time
That bridges the chasm
From the edge of yesterday
To today's shore.

Some of the Characters Cast in Dreams

We see them in the chambers of our sleeping mind
As dashing lovers, idols
As cherished heroes, mentors, foes and rivals
In comedies and tragedies
Of our oneiric life.

And yet, the real human beings
The ones who walk this Earth
And graced us with a cameo role
Upon our dreams
They cannot vouch for anything
We saw, for they weren't really there!

Not one of them could clarify, confirm
Or contradict a scene
Since they were only fleeting images
Reflections in the echo chambers of our mind
Whose image had been borrowed by our memory
To serve our aims without
Their own awareness.

They lived in another universe
Far, far away completely unaware
Of our dream world.

The Books of Life

Biographies account for only parts
Of our existence
They only include two-thirds
Of all our lives
The time when we're awake.

The pictures, documents and letters
That we proffer
Confirm connections with the real world
The places where we lived
The people whom we knew.
And they will vouch for us
Or contradict us if we lie.

What of the other third of our existence
The years we spent asleep which in
A sixty-year span can sum to twenty years?
What book is there for those years?
If there was one, its pages would be blank
As if they had been written with invisible ink.

The marvelous adventures that we dreamed
The shadowy people in preposterous places
Would be all gone, erased as if they never happened
As if its pages had been edited and signed
By sleep's biographer, Oblivion himself.

And Finally, the Why of Dreams

If all those feats I lived
Those epic escapades and cowardly retreats,
Those stellar chats with intellectual oracles,
And those morality plays where guilt
Upbraided me for sins I didn't commit
If all of it was doomed to be forgotten
What was the point of dreaming?

If dreams at times are as absurd
As postcards from a blackhole
Or ski resorts within the sun
What is the point of dreams?

Perhaps the point is living the preposterous
Experiencing a life beyond the comprehension
Of our blasé, jejune real world.
Where else could humans fly like birds?
Or move at the speed of thought?
Where else could we survive being shot
Or walk away from brutal falls as if we were immortal?

For once we are free of obligations
Of gravity constraints, of want and duty,
For once we shirk the grind of competition
The bane of toil, of sweat and hunger.

The poor man feels a millionaire
The blind can see a multi-colored world
The lonely feel the warmth of love.

Don't try to know the point of that.
Just live it, enjoy it and be thankful.

Edward L. Alban (Eddie to friends and colleagues) was born in Ecuador in 1938. He settled in Savannah, Georgia in 1952, and married his wife JoAnn in 1965. They raised two children together. A professor of Economics, he has taught at Auburn University, SUNY Potsdam, Armstrong State University and Savannah State University. He retired in 2000 and has been writing poetry and fiction ever since.

In his retirement, he and JoAnn have traveled throughout Europe and South America, pursuing his new avocation for languages and literature and publishing poetry, fiction and nonfiction. Publications include his epic novel, *Stealing Forbidden Dreams; This Life is So Brief, Between Eternities* (Poetry) and his nonfiction, *Our Gun Idolatry* and *Word Memoirs*.

www.ingramcontent.com/pod-product-compliance
Lightning Source LLC
Chambersburg PA
CBHW051614010526
44107CB00036B/1423/J